The Adventurers

Isabel Anderson

800-445-5985   www.etacuisenaire.com

The Adventurers

ISBN 978-0-7406-1561-0
ETA 303011

ETA/Cuisenaire • Vernon Hills, IL 60061-1862
800-445-5985 • www.etacuisenaire.com

Published by ETA/Cuisenaire® under license from Pearson Education Australia
(a division of Pearson Australia Group Pty Ltd)
All rights reserved.

Text © 2001 Isabel Anderson
Designer: Caroline Laird
Acknowledgments: Cover, title, 15, 27, 28-29, News Limited; 7, AP Photo/Donald
Stampfli; 8-9, AP Photo/Keystone/Fabrice Coffrini; 11, National Air and Space
Museum, Smithsonian Institution (SI Neg. No. A-747-K); 12-13, Getty Images; 16-17,
Australian Picture Library/Corbis; 19, Michael Nichols/NGS Image Collection; 20-21,
M & C Denis Huot-Bios/Auscape; 23, 24-25, AAP Image/Dave Hunt.

Printed in China by QP International Ltd

08 09 10 11 12   10 9 8 7 6 5 4 3

Contents

What Do Adventurers Do?

Adventurers like a challenge. Somewhere in the world you can always find adventurers crossing oceans, climbing mountains, or exploring wild forests.

Balloonists set off to go around the world.

Mountaineers reach top of Mt. Everest.

An explorer treks through wild forest.

The first pilot to cross the Atlantic Ocean sets off.

ATLANTIC OCEAN

PACIFIC OCEAN

A solo rower sets off to cross the Pacific Ocean.

The youngest yachtsman sails around the world.

Balloonists Go Around the World

Who are they? Bertrand Piccard and Brian Jones

What did they do? They were the first people to fly non-stop around the world in a hot-air balloon. They flew more than 28,500 miles.

What did they use? A hot-air balloon called the *Breitling Orbiter 3*

How long did it take? 19 days, 21 hours, and 47 minutes

When did they do it? 1999

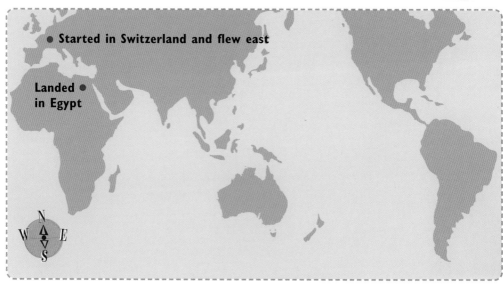

- Started in Switzerland and flew east

Landed • in Egypt

The journey started in Switzerland and ended in the desert in Egypt. (We do not know the exact route they took.)

Cruising in a Capsule

Piccard and Jones didn't travel in a basket attached to the balloon. They traveled in a special capsule. Here they are at the entrance to the capsule.

To fly around the world, balloons have to fly high to avoid bad weather that could slow them down. The capsule gave the pilots the oxygen they needed to breathe in thin air. It kept them warm, too.

Help on Board

You might think it would be lonely flying high in the sky in a balloon, but Piccard and Jones were never alone. They could use a special phone to contact their support team on the ground. They used navigation and communication equipment to find their way across the skies. Cameras on board helped them to navigate.

Here is the *Breitling Orbiter 3* balloon flying over the Swiss Alps. This photo was taken soon after the balloon was launched.

Flight Rules

One of the rules of the flight was that the balloon couldn't land along the way. If it did, then equipment on the balloon would have shown this!

Pilot Crosses the Atlantic

Who was he? Charles Lindbergh
What did he do? He made the first non-stop flight across the Atlantic Ocean.
What did he use? A plane called the *Spirit of St. Louis*
How long did it take? 33½ hours to fly 3,600 miles
When did he do it? 1927

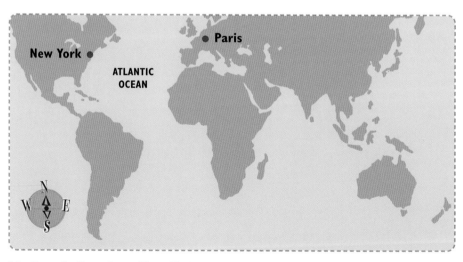

Lindbergh flew from New York to Paris, France.

When Lindbergh flew non-stop for more than 30 hours, he sat in an ordinary wicker chair in a tiny cockpit. The chair was chosen because it was lightweight. The plane had to be as light as possible to allow Lindbergh to carry more fuel. To fly the longest distance ever, Lindbergh needed a lot of fuel.

In 1927, airplanes were flimsy machines made of wire and wood. They weren't carrying people and cargo all over the world, like airplanes do today.

The *Spirit of St. Louis* was built especially for the journey across the Atlantic. This journey was the longest ever flown without stopping.

Lindbergh didn't have radio contact with anyone. He fought against tiredness, constantly forcing himself to stay awake.

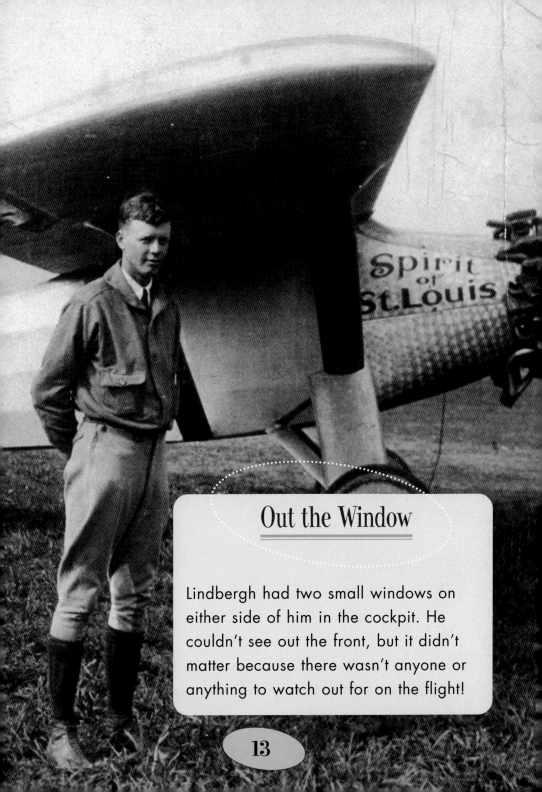

Out the Window

Lindbergh had two small windows on either side of him in the cockpit. He couldn't see out the front, but it didn't matter because there wasn't anyone or anything to watch out for on the flight!

Mountaineers Reach the Top

Who are they? Edmund Hillary and Tenzing Norgay
What did they do? They were the first people to climb to the top of Mt. Everest, the highest mountain in the world. Mt. Everest is 29,028 feet high.
How long did it take? About 2 months
When did they do it? 1953

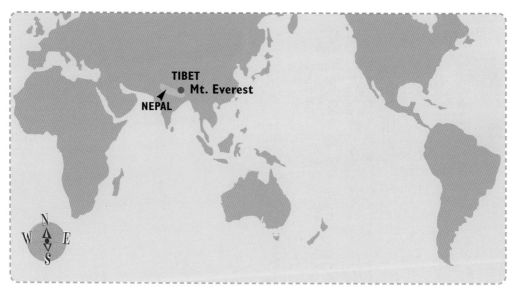

Mt. Everest is on the border between Nepal and Tibet.

In 1953, a team of mountain climbers set out to conquer Mt. Everest. Since the 1920s, climbers had unsuccessfully tried to reach its summit. This team was led by John Hunt, who worked out a plan for a successful climb. Hunt chose the climbers for the team. They needed to be strong, fit, experienced in icy conditions, and be able to work well as a team. Edmund Hillary and Tenzing Norgay were included on the team.

This is Tenzing Norgay and Edmund Hillary after their successful climb. Norgay was an experienced local mountaineer. He was a Sherpa. The Sherpa people come from northeastern Nepal and are familiar with mountain conditions.

What did they take with them?

The team took thousands of yards of rope for climbing, tools such as axes for breaking ice, and stoves for cooking. They also took oxygen equipment. When people climb high up in the mountains, the air contains less oxygen. You need oxygen to breathe properly.

Who Will Carry It?

The team hired 350 people to carry their equipment into the mountains!

Two at the Top

It was a team effort, but only two climbers conquered
Mt. Everest. As they neared the summit, Hillary and Norgay
spent long hours using their axes to make steps in the ice.
They used these steps to climb. They also kept an eye on the
amount of oxygen left in the tanks they carried on their backs.

Explorer Treks Through Wild Forest

Who is he? Michael Fay
What did he do? He walked across parts of Africa that people hadn't lived in for over 100 years.
How long did it take? 460 days to walk 1,240 miles
When did he do it? 1999–2000

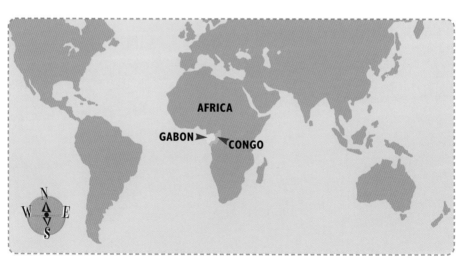

The journey took Fay through the forests of the Congo to the beaches of Gabon.

Here Fay is paddling through a swamp. He is wearing a headlamp to see where he is going. Can you see the light trails from the headlamp?

Fay's journey took him through the last stretch of undisturbed forest in Africa. No human had been in the forest for more than 100 years. When Fay was faced with a charging elephant, he believed it was likely that the elephant had never seen humans before!

Keeping Records

Fay is a conservationist, and he made records of his trip in 87 waterproof notebooks. He hoped that these records would show how important this wilderness area is and that it needs to be preserved. Fay kept a video record of his journey, too.

Help on the Way

Fay made this journey with ten local people to help him. He used a wrist compass and a navigational system to guide him.

Fay's group encountered many animals, including leopards, chimpanzees, and hippopotamuses. Fay discovered that the hippos come out of the forests and relax on the beach in Gabon!

Rower Crosses the Pacific

Who is he? Jim Shekhdar

What did he do? He was the first person to row across the Pacific Ocean without help.

What did he use? A 20-foot rowboat named *Le Shark*

How long did it take? 8 months to row 8,000 miles

When did he do it? 2001

PACIFIC OCEAN

PERU

SOUTH AMERICA

AUSTRALIA

N W E S

Shekhdar started his journey in Peru in South America. He rowed across the Pacific Ocean to reach Australia.

A Big Boat

The rowboat that Shekhdar used was no ordinary rowboat.
It was much larger than a normal rowboat in order to carry
navigation and communication equipment. Shekhdar could
use the navigation equipment to find his location. He could
use the communication equipment to send short messages.

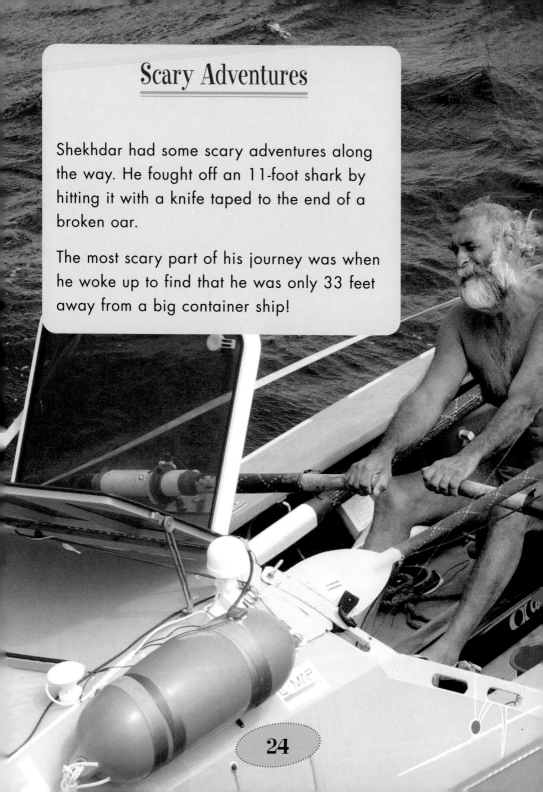

Scary Adventures

Shekhdar had some scary adventures along the way. He fought off an 11-foot shark by hitting it with a knife taped to the end of a broken oar.

The most scary part of his journey was when he woke up to find that he was only 33 feet away from a big container ship!

Rowing in the Rough

Shekhdar wore a harness in rough weather. It kept him from slipping around in the boat and from falling overboard in rough waters.

Youngest Yachtsman
Sails Around the World

Youngest Yachtsman
Sails Around the World

Who is he? Jesse Martin
What did he do? He is the youngest person to sail non-stop completely around the world on his own.
What did he use? A 36-foot yacht named the *Lionheart*
How long did it take? 11 months to sail 31,000 miles
When did he do it? 1998–1999

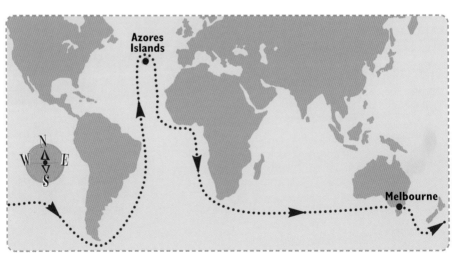

Martin's journey started in Melbourne, Australia, and went east. To circumnavigate the world, he needed to pass around the Azores Islands, which are on the exact opposite side of the earth from Melbourne.

Here Martin is setting out on his journey.

Martin's yacht was called the *Lionheart*. It was specially built to be stronger than other yachts and to hold all the supplies that Martin needed for such a long journey. There was so much extra equipment on Martin's boat that it sailed lower in the water than a normal boat.

Sleeping on the Job

Martin could sleep no more than twenty minutes at a time. He had to stay awake to watch out for passing ships that might collide with his boat. In the South Atlantic Ocean, he was hit, but it wasn't by a ship. The boat was hit by a whale!

Sometimes the yacht was battered by huge waves. The temperature also got as low as 4 degrees Fahrenheit for long periods of time. Martin used up a lot of his energy keeping warm, staying awake, and just concentrating on what he needed to do to sail the yacht.

Staying Clean

Martin had to be very careful with water. He could only use a cup of water a day to wash in.

Whose Adventure?

Match the adventurers with their adventure.

Edmund Hillary and Tenzing Norgay	First flight across the Atlantic Ocean
Jesse Martin	First to reach the top of Mt. Everest
Charles Lindbergh	First non-stop balloon flight around the world
Bertrand Piccard and Brian Jones	First solo rowboat to cross the Pacific Ocean
Jim Shekhdar	Youngest solo yacht journey around the world

Glossary

capsule   enclosed space that's attached to, but separate from, a balloon

cargo   things that are carried on a plane

circumnavigate   sail completely around something

cockpit   part of the plane where the pilot sits

conservationist   person who wants to take care of the environment

research projects   investigations to find information

solo   done alone

yacht   private sailing boat

Index